The GHOST Hunter's Guide

KT-384-569

Charles Bouvier

EDGE
FRANKLIN WATTS

Bromley Libraries

30128 80062 573 6

Ever lain in bed at night, listening to the floorboards creak as the wood moves and groans. Or heard a branch scraping against the window, almost like the long nails of an ancient hand? Deep down, you've probably wondered if that's what they really are...

Ghosts, spirits, wraiths – whatever you call them, they are talked about and feared all around the world. From phantom armies to the terrifying yurei of Japan, the White Ladies of the Philippines, the vengeful ghosts bent on luring others to their deaths, and many more, this book tells you how to recognise, and deal with, all kinds of ghost.

Good luck!

Charles Bouvier

CONTENTS

Words in bold are in the glossary

Ghosts everywhere!

All around the world as night falls, people tell stories of ghosts. Some ghosts are frightening, but harmless. Others can suck the life out of you, or terrify you into madness.

"She materialised right next to me and she looked like a white mist vaguely in the shape of an old lady. She touched me first on my hand then up on to my arm, and both places she touched me became as cold as ice."

– Account of a haunted grocery shop from 1980.

Hunting ghosts

Ghost hunters are a ghost's worst nightmare. They try to track down these **incorporeal** spirits, before destroying or banishing them. It takes nerves of steel to be a ghost hunter – we are not all brave enough to pursue ghosts through dusty buildings and lonely woods!

▼ It's always fun telling ghost stories round a campfire – but are you brave enough to go on a ghost hunt afterwards?

Becoming a ghost hunter

How do you fight a ghost – a creature that can disappear through walls and vanish through closed doors? This book will start you on the path to becoming a ghost hunter.
You'll discover:

- How to spot the ghosts that are dangerous.
- The powers ghosts use against their victims.
- Ways to stay safe from ghosts, fight them, and perhaps even destroy them.

▼ *Would you be a dedicated enough ghost hunter to visit this spooky house – at night?*

Ghost-hunting kit

Your ghost-hunting kit doesn't need to be expensive. You probably already have many of the things on this list:

- Camera (photo and video)
- Sound recorder
- Sealable plastic bags for evidence
- Compass (it starts twitching if there is ghostly energy nearby)
- Talcum powder (for sprinkling and detecting ghostly footprints)
- Thermometer (for confirming falls in temperature).

Ghosts, spirits and revenants

It isn't just the names for ghosts that are different: there are lots of different types of ghost, too. Not all of them are dangerous, so which ones should you keep a special watch for?

Which are the most dangerous ghosts?

The most dangerous ghosts are called **revenants**. These are spirits of the dead that have returned to haunt the living. The two main reasons why they come back are:

• Those who have died in tragic accidents may return to haunt the scene – either to warn people, or to lure them towards a similar ending.

• Murder victims whose murderer has gone unpunished may return for revenge.

◄ Reaching out from beyond the grave, some ghosts are determined to do harm to the living.

Dangerous spirits

Around the world, there are plenty of other dangerous ghosts. There are spirits with magical powers and long, sharp teeth. There are 'Hungry Ghosts', which have their own special festival each year to stop them from harming the living. And ghost ships, ghost riders and even ghost armies are regularly spotted. So there's plenty to keep a ghost hunter busy!

HAUNTED PLACES

Certain places seem to attract ghosts. For example:
• Beechworth Lunatic Asylum, Australia – haunted by the ghosts of former patients
• Old Ford Motor Factory, Singapore – home to mysterious noises and lights at night
• Union Cemetery, Connecticut, USA (below) – haunted by a White Lady (see pages 10–11), among others.

◄ At the Day of the Dead festival in Mexico, people honour their **ancestors** in the hope that it will stop them from becoming revenants.

▼ Union Cemetery in Connecticut, USA, is said to be one of the most haunted places in North America.

Lemures of ancient Rome

Imagine that you're walking along the dark streets of ancient Rome at night. You're on the lookout for robbers, when you catch sight of something in the corner of your eye. Spinning round, you look towards it – but there's nothing there. Could it be… a lemure?

Ghost Fact File

Name: Lemure
Location: Roman Empire
Age: 2,500 years

▼ The Forum in Rome, Italy, lay at the heart of the city. Thousands of years ago, it was dark and deserted at night. Few dared to cross it for fear of lemures.

Appearance and behaviour

Lemures can be felt most strongly at night. They take no form, and can only be sensed in the shadows, from the corner of your eye. If they are not banished, they can cause all kinds of trouble:

- Bad luck in business or friendships
- Crops failing or food stores going bad
- Sickness, and even death.

Banishing lemures

Lemures are best dealt with on 9, 11 and 13 May. These are the days when Roman fathers would wait until midnight to scatter handfuls of black beans around the home. The lemures ate the beans, and were satisfied. Any that remained could be scared off by banging bronze pots together.

▲ *Farmers in ancient Rome carried out ceremonies to keep lemures away.*

Roman father: "I send these; with these beans I redeem me and mine." (*Repeat nine times*)

Rest of household (clashing bronze pots together): "Ghosts of my fathers and ancestors, be gone!" (*Repeat nine times*)

- Ceremony for banishing lemures in ancient Rome

9

The White Lady

On lonely roads and paths, late at night, it pays to look out for a White Lady. These mysterious ghosts are unlikely to cause you harm. Instead, they give a warning that something terrible is about to happen.

Ghost Fact File

Name: White Lady
Location: Worldwide
Age: Not known

White Ladies are the ghosts of women who have suffered a tragic death, often after being treated badly by the man they loved. They are often associated with a particular family, and appear before a disaster; usually a death.

▼ White Lady ghosts appear suddenly on remote, lonely pathways and roads.

▼ *This lonely road in Wyoming, USA is said to have been visited by a White Lady.*

Appearance

It is rare to see a White Lady close up, but from a distance they look exactly as you would imagine. They are pale, ghostly women, wearing loose white clothes. White Ladies usually look slightly blurry, especially around the edges.

Behaviour

White Ladies rarely hurt the people who see them. Some, having been treated badly by men when alive, are not that keen on male company. If they meet men who remind them of the one they loved, they can get very annoyed.

WHITE LADIES AROUND THE WORLD

White Lady ghosts appear in many places:
- Berry Pomeroy Castle in Devon, UK
- Mullaghmoyle Road in County Tyrone, Ireland
- Old Faithful Inn in Wyoming, USA (this White Lady has the bonus of being headless)
- Balete Drive, Manila, the Philippines.

Ghost hitchhikers

Imagine yourself in a car on a lonely road, late at night. Suddenly, through the mist and rain, you see a hitchhiker. You pull over, and the hitcher climbs in. But everything is not as it seems. You've just picked up a ghost hitchhiker!

▼ What was that at the side of the road? It may be safer not to stop to find out!

Appearance

Ghost hitchhikers look just like any other hitchhiker. But if you meet one, you will probably sense something strange about them. They may not speak much, look pale and ill, or have a strange smell.

RESURRECTION MARY

Mary is the ghost of a young woman buried in Resurrection Cemetery in Chicago, USA. She died after being hit by a car on her way home from a party. Drivers take pity on Mary because she wears only a thin white ball gown. Once in the car, she says nothing until it passes Resurrection Cemetery. "Stop here!" she shouts, then disappears into the graveyard. Only then does the driver realise whom they had picked up....

Behaviour

Different ghost hitchhikers rarely behave in exactly the same way. But here are three things that they might do:

- Disappear from the car the moment it arrives where the hitcher asked to be dropped off.
- Get out of the car normally, but leave something behind. When the driver knocks on the door of the house where the hitcher was dropped off, he or she is told that the object belonged to someone who has died.
- Make a **prophecy** of a terrible event, before vanishing into thin air.

▲ If the Sun's still up, it's probably a real person hoping for a lift – not a ghost! Very few ghost hitchhikers appear in daylight.

Ghostly crashes

Not all ghost hitchhikers are spooky but harmless. Some evil ghosts seem determined to cause car crashes. There have been many reports of ghosts suddenly appearing in the middle of the road, causing a car to swerve and crash.

▼ Watch out for ghosts that suddenly appear on a lonely road at night. They are said to cause many accidents.

Yurei of Japan

Night-time travellers in the forests of Japan should watch out for strange flames that seem to float and flicker through the trees. They may show that a **vengeful**, ghostly yurei is nearby.

Ghost Fact File

Name: Yurei
Location: Japan
Age: Several thousand
     years

A yurei is the spirit of a dead person which can bridge the gap between the **Afterlife** and the physical world. It may come back for revenge, or because of jealousy, hatred or grief. Or it may have been trapped between the two worlds by not having had a proper burial, being murdered or dying in tragic circumstances.

Appearance

The yurei almost always appear dressed in white, and have long, black messy hair. Their hands dangle from their wrists, and their arms are held out in front of them, like sleepwalkers. They do not need feet or legs, as they move by floating silently through the air.

▲ *Could that flickering light between the trees be a yurei?*

▲ *A yurei appears before his family, demanding that his spirit be able to rest in peace.*

CATEGORIES OF YUREI

Not all yurei are dangerous:

Dangerous! Onry, who have returned for revenge
Safe! Ubume, mothers who return to look after their children
Dangerous! Funayurei, the ghosts of those who have died at sea
Naughty! Zashiki-warashi, the mischievous ghosts of children

Behaviour

Yurei are most likely to be seen between 2 and 3 o'clock in the morning, when the barriers between the worlds of the living and the dead are thinnest. They appear near to places linked to their death. A yurei who was murdered, for example, will haunt the place where he or she was killed.

There is only one way to get rid of a yurei: put right whatever caused them to return to the world of the living in the first place. Even then, particularly strong yurei may continue to haunt a place for a long time afterwards.

Rakshasa of India

If there's one spirit even the bravest ghost hunter really doesn't want to run into, it is a rakshasa. This spirit from India occupies a physical body. It has a fearsome appearance, poisonous fingernails, and is said to be able to **shape-shift**. If you come across a Rakshasa, you'd better run away – fast!

What is a rakshasa?

No one is certain where rakshasas come from. Many people agree, however, that the most dangerous rakshasas are the spirits of those who lived particularly wicked lives.

▲ *The crazy staring eyes and fangs are a big clue: this is a rakshasa.*

Appearance

Rakshasas are always terrifying-looking, though they do not all look the same. Some have ten heads. Others have long, sharp teeth, or are six metres tall. All, though, are scary enough to make the blood drain from your face. And they are spectacularly bad tempered.

"Rakshasa is the [follower] of Ravana. Ravana, whose deeds were so horrible they stopped the Sun and Moon in their course."

– from *Kolchak: The Night Stalker* (1974)

Behaviour

Generally, rakshasas are not very well behaved. Their favourite activities include:

- Making a mess of graves.
- Eating human flesh.
- Taking **possession** of human beings and making them perform evil acts.
- Disrupting religious ceremonies.

Each rakshasa has magical powers, and is a master of illusion. This makes them extremely hard to beat – though Hindu stories do tell of the defeat of the rakshasa leader Ravana and his followers in a great battle.

▼ *Rakshasas are the followers of Ravana, the Hindu demon, who snarls out from this carving.*

Noisy spirits

You're in a house investigating a haunting. Suddenly, a heavy chair starts to move across the room. It stops, but then there's a noise of banging from the kitchen – a room with no one in it. Finally, an invisible hand throws a book at your head. It's time to leave! You've stumbled across a poltergeist.

AMITYVILLE

In 1975, a family called Lutz moved into a house in Amityville, New York, USA. A year earlier, the house had been the scene of a terrible murder.

Terrifying events began to happen:
• Swarms of flies would appear.
• Red eyes were seen looking out of the windows.
• Green slime oozed from the walls, and through keyholes.

The events were blamed on a poltergeist. In January 1976, the Lutz family moved out, and never returned.

▲ The house at 112 Ocean Drive, where the Amityville haunting is said to have taken place.

▲ A scene from the 1982 film Poltergeist, in which a young girl is haunted by ancient ghosts.

Appearance

Poltergeists are rarely visible. You will know that there is a poltergeist around though. Poltergeist means 'noisy spirit', and this ghost certainly makes itself heard. Strange noises are common when there's a poltergeist around, including mysterious footsteps, the sound of furniture being moved in empty rooms and unexplained crashes and bangs.

Behaviour

Poltergeists are known as evil spirits, rather than ghosts. They are often linked to a particular human, usually a young woman, who is responsible for the poltergeist's actions. They are usually, though not always, associated with a particular place. Poltergeists are angry, disruptive ghosts. They throw things around, make a lot of noise and mess, and may even attack people.

Getting rid of a poltergeist

Poltergeists usually appear suddenly, and disappear just as quickly. People have tried using a religious ceremony called **exorcism** to get rid of poltergeists. Usually, though, the poltergeist eventually goes away of its own accord.

Ghost ship: The Flying Dutchman

You might think that the last thing sailors want to spot far out at sea is a terrible storm approaching. In fact, that's the second last thing. The very LAST thing sailors want to see is a ghost ship called the *Flying Dutchman*.

Ghost Fact File

Name: *The Flying Dutchman*
Location: Any ocean
Age: At least 300 years

A dreadful omen

The Dutchman, as sailors call it, is known to be a **harbinger** of bad luck. Some kind of dreadful disaster or accident always befalls those who see it – usually a shipwreck. That's why sailors hope to never see the *Flying Dutchman* appear on the horizon.

◄ *An old painting showing the* Flying Dutchman *(far left) luring a sailing ship to its doom on the rocks.*

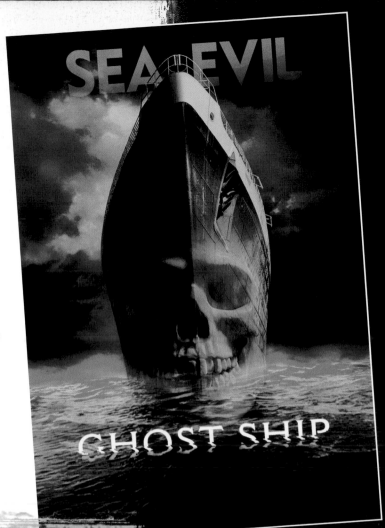

SEA EVIL

GHOST SHIP

► *The 2002 movie Ghost Ship, in which people are trapped on a ship, was partly inspired by the legend of the Flying Dutchman.*

THE LEGEND of the FLYING DUTCHMAN

The *Flying Dutchman* was commanded by Captain Van der Drecken. When the captain was asked to put into port instead of continuing to fight a fierce wind off South Africa, he replied: "I will round this Cape even if I have to keep sailing till **Doomsday**!" Soon after, the ship was wrecked, but Van der Drecken's ghost ship is still said to sail the seas, and will do so until the world ends.

Appearance and behaviour

The *Flying Dutchman* is a sailing ship from the 1700s. According to legend, it was wrecked while sailing around the stormy Cape of Good Hope off South Africa. From a distance, it glows with a ghostly light.

The whole ship appears wrecked. Despite its shredded sails, the *Flying Dutchman* is often reported sailing against the wind, as if driven by some magical power.

Phantom armies

There is a scene in the film trilogy *The Lord of the Rings* where one of the characters summons a **phantom** army to help him in a great battle. Of course, *The Lord of the Rings* is based on a story – but there have been plenty of reports of phantom armies in real life, too.

Appearance

It is usually possible to tell that you are looking at a ghost army, rather than a real one. They often come from an earlier time, and are dressed differently from modern soldiers. But some ghost armies are very convincing. In 1746, villagers near Souter **Fell** in England fled from an army of Scottish soldiers invading England – only to realise later that it was a ghost army.

◄ *A ghostly army appears out of the misty forest. How could you defeat such enemies, when they're already dead?*

Behaviour

Ghost armies generally limit their activities to appearing and disappearing. But some are said to have taken part in actual fighting:

• Ghost armies twice saved the Italian city of Otranto from capture by Turkish forces. When the city was attacked in 1537 and 1644, the ghosts of 800 soldiers killed in an earlier battle with the Turks appeared.

• During the Battle of Mons (part of the First World War 1914–18), a force of spirits rescued English soldiers from certain death by startling the horses of their German attackers, giving the English a chance to escape.

▼ Spooky Denbigh Moors is said to be regularly visited by ghost armies.

Civil War armies

Phantom armies have appeared at battle sites from the English **Civil War** (1642–51), and the American Civil War (1861–65). They include:

• Edgehill, Naseby, and Roundway Down in England

• Shiloh in Tennessee in the USA, where there are regular reports of phantom armies and mysterious sounds of battle.

THE HAUNTED MOOR

Denbigh Moors, in north Wales, is said to be haunted both by a ghostly Roman **centurion**, and a 3,000-strong army from the 1800s. It's a spooky place: strange noises, odd lights and UFOs have all been reported there too.

China's Hungry Ghost festival

Ghost Fact File

Name: Hungry Ghost
Location: China and South-
East Asia
Age: At least 2,000 years

▲ *People burn offerings to the spirits to celebrate the Hungry Ghost festival.*

The seventh month of the Chinese calendar is a great time for a ghost hunter to visit China. For the whole month, dead souls return to the world of the living as ghosts.

Some of these ghosts may be 'hungry' – wanting something from the living. Unless they are kept happy, they may cause bad luck, sickness or even unexpected deaths. The Hungry Ghost festival aims to make the ghosts contented, so that they bring good luck instead of bad.

The most ghostly day

On the fifteenth day of the seventh month, according to Chinese legend, the gates between Heaven, Hell and the world of the living are wide open and ghosts can pass between them. There are several ways to keep the wandering ghosts from causing harm:

• Putting on shows to entertain them (but NEVER sit in the front row – it's reserved for ghosts!).
• Preparing complicated meals, with places set for dead ancestors.
• Burning paper models of golden materials, fine clothes, fake paper money, and other precious things, as gifts to the dead.

"People pray for their dead ancestors and hope they do not come up to haunt them or their loved ones. They are also very careful in doing almost anything [risky], i.e. no fast driving, no swimming, etc."

— Felix from Taiwan.

GHOST FESTIVALS AROUND THE WORLD

Although the Hungry Ghost festival is Chinese, it is also celebrated in Japan (where it is called O-bon), Vietnam (Tét Trung Nguyên) and around the world in countries with large Chinese communities.

► *Chinese god Hu Fa Shi Zhe is an important spirit to keep happy – he is the controller of ghosts and devils.*

All Hallows' Eve

All Hallows' Eve is usually called Halloween. People dress up in costumes and go trick-or-treating, knocking on doors in the hope that they'll be given sweets. But All Hallows' Eve has a much more sinister, ghostly past.

▼ *Halloween has been the subject of plenty of horror movies.*

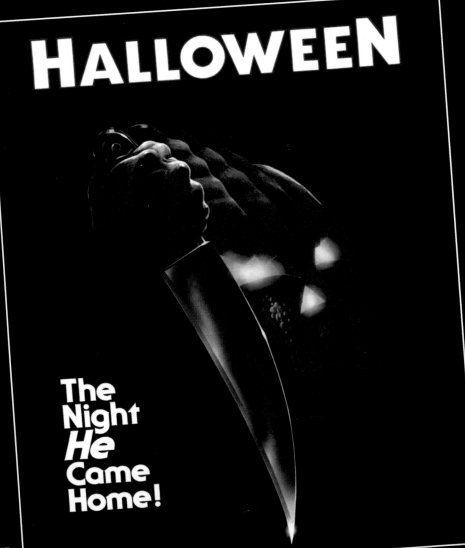

HALLOWEEN

The Night He Came Home!

For centuries, people have known that on All Hallows' Eve, the walls between the worlds of the living and the dead are at their thinnest. This is when evil spirits are free to visit the world of the living.

Trick-or-treating

When you knock on someone's door trick-or-treating, you're continuing an ancient tradition. It started many years ago, when poor people would call at the homes of the rich, asking for food. In return they would pray for the souls of the dead, so that they did not come back to haunt the living.

Halloween costumes

Dressing up in scary costumes is a kind of 'guising'. 'Guising' means disguising yourself as a ghost or demon in the hope that you will fool the evil sprits into thinking you are one of them so they will leave you alone.

Jack o'lanterns

Jack o'lanterns are traditionally lit on Halloween. They are a reminder of Stingy Jack, a miserly Irish farmer who tried to cheat on a deal with the Devil. As a result he was cursed to wander the Earth forever, using a candle inside a hollowed-out turnip to light his way.

"Tis now the very witching time of night,

When churchyards yawn and hell itself breathes out

Contagion to this world."

- from *Hamlet* (William Shakespeare)

▼ *Old stories say that snaggle-toothed lanterns like these are lit on All Hallows' Eve to keep wandering evil spirits like Stingy Jack away.*

Ghosts on screen

Nearly everyone enjoys feeling scared once in a while – as long as we're not too scared! And one of the best ways to get your scary thrills is to go to see a ghost movie.

Old-school films

Old ghost movies were made in the days before filmmakers could really use special effects. Instead, the audience had to imagine what might be creeping up on the actors. Some of the best movies include:

• *The Uninvited* (1944) – a brother and sister buy a mysterious, abandoned house, and strange things start to happen…

• *The Haunting* (1963) – the simple story of four guests invited to spend the night in a house, to prove that ghosts and spirits do not exist. Of course, it turns out that perhaps they do…

▶ *A scary scene from one of the best ghost movies of all time* – The Haunting.

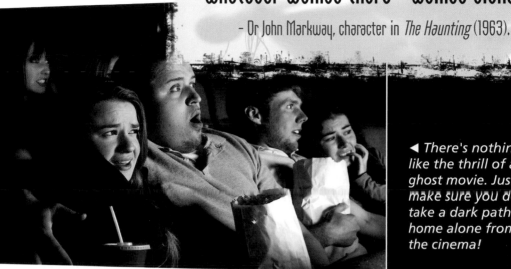

"An evil old house, the kind some people call haunted... Silence lay steadily against the wood and stone of Hill House, and whatever walked there – walked alone."

– Dr John Markway, character in *The Haunting* (1963).

◄ *There's nothing like the thrill of a ghost movie. Just make sure you don't take a dark path home alone from the cinema!*

▲ *In* Sleepy Hollow *Constable Ichabod Crane gets tangled up with the ghostly Headless Horseman.*

Modern ghost movies

Modern ghost movies are sometimes quite bloodthirsty. But there are some great films that manage to be scary without being too gory:

• *The Sixth Sense* (1999) – the story of a young boy who sees and speaks with ghosts.

• *Ghostbusters* (1984) – not so much scary as funny, this movie tells the story of a team of crack ghost hunters and their efforts to stop evil spirits destroying the world.

• *Sleepy Hollow* (1998) – the story of police constable Ichabod Crane, and his attempts to get rid of the Headless Horseman.

Technical information

Words from this book:

Afterlife
place where the spirits of the dead go.

ancestor
person who lived a long time ago.

centurion
soldier in the army of ancient Rome.

civil war
war fought between two sides who are from the same country.

contagion
harm and decay.

Doomsday
in Christian beliefs, the day at the end of the world when people will be judged and sent to heaven or hell.

exorcism
religious ceremony to get rid of ghosts.

fell
area of high ground.

harbinger
messenger or announcer.

incorporeal
without a body.

phantom
old word for a ghost or spirit.

possession
control or ownership.

prophecy
a forecast or prediction. Ghosts, with their connections to the spirit world, seem to be able to know the future as well as the past, and sometimes make prophecies.

revenant
spirit of a dead person, which has returned to the world of the living (often to avenge an injustice).

shape-shift
change shape or form.

vengeful
wanting to take revenge.

Equipment:

Basic ghost-hunting equipment is listed on page 5. The following items are more specialist, and may be very expensive. They're for expert ghost trackers only!

Electromagnetic frequency (EMF) detector – these pick up electronic fields (which may be given off by ghosts) at various frequencies.

Infrared scanner (hand-held) – this picks up infrared light. Some ghosts may be seen using infrared light, or may give it off.

Night-vision equipment – goggles help you to see what's happening in the dark; night-vision cameras will record events.

More ghostly information

Other books

Ghosts and Monsters: Frightening Phantoms and Supernatural Spooks (Ticktock Books, 2006)
Collected information about all kinds of ghosts, plus other supernatural events.

Encyclopedia Horrifica: The Terrifying Truth About Vampires, Ghosts, Monsters and More Joshua Gee (Scholastic, 2007)
Not just ghosts, but all kinds of supernatural and paranormal creatures and events, are covered in this book.

The Encyclopedia of the Unexplained Judy Allen (Kingfisher, 2006)
Although the section on ghosts doesn't take up much of this book, it's still a good read. The rest, which deals with mysteries such as crop circles and the Bermuda Triangle, is really interesting too!

Although the following are adult titles, they would be useful to confident readers who want to find out more:

The Mammoth Book of True Hauntings & The Mammoth Book of Haunted House Stories both Peter Haining (Robinson, 2008)
These books are absolutely jam-packed with examples of hundreds of hauntings from around the world.

The Paranormal: Caught On Film Melvyn Willin (David & Charles, 2008)
Some brilliant photographs of what may, or may not, be ghosts.

The Internet

www.monstropedia.org
This is a great, big rambling site, which is absolutely full of information about all kinds of weird, supernatural and scary creatures. To get to the ghosts section, click on 'Paranormal entities', then 'Ghosts'.

www.ghostresearch.org/ghostpics/
This site is great fun – some maybe-ghost photos, and some that everyone admits are fakes, with explanations of how they can be faked. Click on 'Typical website frauds' for some especially good ones.

Movies and DVDs

Beetlejuice (1988, dir. Tim Burton)
A darkly funny film about a dead couple who decide to hang around their old house in order to scare away the new inhabitants.

Ghostbusters (1984, dir. Ivan Reitman)
A humorous film about a trio of men who set up a business ridding New York of its ghosts and ghouls.

Note to parents and teachers: every effort has been made by the Publishers to ensure that these websites are suitable for children, that they are of the highest educational value, and that they contain no inappropriate or offensive material. However, because of the nature of the Internet, it is impossible to guarantee that the contents of these sites will not be altered. We strongly advise that Internet access is supervised by a responsible adult.

Index

First published in 2012 by
Franklin Watts
338 Euston Road
London NW1 3BH

Franklin Watts Australia
Level 17/207 Kent Street
Sydney NSW 2000

Copyright © Franklin Watts 2011

All rights reserved.

Series editors: Adrian Cole and Julia Bird
Art director: Jonathan Hair
Design: Mayer Media
Picture research: Diana Morris

ISBN 978 1 4451 0122 4

Dewey number: 113.1

A CIP catalogue record for this book
is available from the British Library.

Printed in China

Franklin Watts is a division of
Hachette Children's Books,
an Hachette UK company.
www.hachette.co.uk

Acknowledgements:
Art Archive: 22b. Asia Images Group/Alamy: 16b. Blitznetsov/
Shutterstock: 1, 4c, 6, 9b, 17c, 25t, 29t. Sascha Burkard/
istockphoto: 5t, 7tr, 11t, 11b, 12b,15b, 23c, 25c. Jeff Chiasson/
istockphoto: 29c. Compass International/Kobal Collection:
26b. Mary Evans PL/Alamy: 15t. Ekaterina Fribus /Shutterstock:
27. Eddie Gerald/Alamy: 13t. Jpse Gil/Shutterstock: 7c. Chris
Harvey/Fotolia: front cover. Chris Hellier/Alamy: 25b. Roger
Holmes/Getty Images: 23b. Iconspro/Shutterstock: 2. Ivancovlad/
Shutterstock: 8c, 10t, 14c, 16t, 20t, 24t. Neal & Molly Jansen/
Alamy: 10b. Geoffrey Jewett/Shutterstock: 4tl, 8tl, 12tl,
14tl, 18tl, 22tl, 26tl. Rob Johnson: 7b. P Kirill /Shutterstock:
12c. Natalia Lukiyanova/frenta/Shutterstock: 3. Maodesign/
istockphoto: 5b. MGM/AF Archive/Alamy: 19t. MGM/Kobal
Collection: 28. Syamsui Bahri Muhammad/Getty Images: 24b.
North Wind PA/Alamy: 20b.Graham Oliver/Alamy: 17b. Silvia
Otte/Getty Images: 8b. Paramount/Mandalay/Kobal Collection:
29b. Picturepoint/Topham: 18b. David Ponton/Corbis: 14b.
Quavondo/istockphoto: 13b. Corey Rich/Aurora Photos/Alamy:
4b. Warner Brothers/Kobal Collection: 21t. Gari Wyn Williams/
Alamy: 9c.

Every attempt has been made to clear copyright.
Should there be any inadvertent omission please
apply to the publisher for rectification.